Mr Trout is Out and About

Written by **Peter Millett**
Illustrated by **Constanza Basaluzzo**

Fast phonics

Before reading this book, ask the student to practise saying the sounds (phonemes) and reading the new words used in the book. Try to make it as speedy and as fun as possible.

Read the tricky high frequency words

The student can't sound out these words at the moment, but they need to know them because they are commonly used.

house   goes   here

Tip: Encourage the student to sound out any sounds they know in these words, and you can provide them with the irregular or tricky part.

Say the sounds

ou cloud   **ow** cow

a-e plane   **i-e** bike   **o-e** cone

ew stew   **ue** rescue   **u** unicorn   **u-e** cube

ew screw   **ue** blue   **ui** fruit   **u-e** flute

Tip: Remember to say the pure sounds. For example, 'ssss' and 'nnnn'. If you need a reminder, watch the *Snappy Sounds* videos.

Snappy words

Point at a word randomly and have the student read the word. The student will need to sound out the word and blend the sounds to read the word. For example: 'c–lll–ow–nnn, clown'.

out	about	trout
town	clown	howl
found	crowds	around
brown	down	ground
shout	crouch	proud
outside	our	clouds
mounts	mouth	south
sound	loudly	round

Quick vocabulary check

The underlined words may not be familiar to the student. Check their understanding before you start to read the book.

Look! It's Mr Trout, our town clown.

He is out and about. He is up and down and all around the town!

The crowds found him outside his house. They howl, shout and jump about.

Mr Trout skates around at the top of a ramp. He looks out and down.

It is higher than a big house.

Mr Trout will crouch down and then shoot into the air.

The crowd on the ground shouts, "Wow!"

When he lands down on the ground, Mr Trout feels proud.

The crowd claps loudly when Mr Trout goes round and round. Then he goes down into the pool.

When Mr Trout grabs a flower out of his robe by the pool, the crowd shouts, "How?"

Mr Trout mounts a brown clown bike.
He rides it to the top of the wheel.

Mr Trout is a long way off the ground.
He can see his house from here!

The crowd shouts, "Wow" and "Don't look down!"

But Mr Trout cannot hear a sound.
He just keeps going round and round.

Then Mr Trout goes up into the sky.
He looks at the clouds as they go by.

Mr Trout jumps out and feels the wind in his mouth as he drops south. As he gets near to the ground, the crowd sounds loud.

"Look, here he comes!" the people in the crowd say aloud.

Mr Trout lands on the ground.

The crowd shouts, "Wow!", and Mr Trout takes a bow.

It is about time for Mr Trout to go home.

He goes back to his house to sit on his couch!

On his couch, Mr Trout plans his next big day. He will go out and about and up and down!

He is Mr Trout, the town clown.

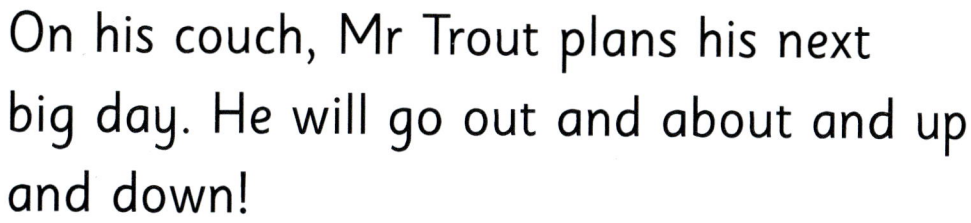

Comprehension questions

Well done!

Let's talk about the story together

Ask the student:
- What was Mr Trout's first trick? What was his last trick?
- Where was Mr Trout when he saw the clouds go by?
- What is another word for 'crouch'?
- Which of Mr Trout's tricks was the best? Why do you think that?

Snappy words

Ask the student to read these words as quickly as they can.

found	around	ground
shout	trout	proud
about	out	crouch

Fluency

Can the student read the story again and improve on the last time?

Have fun!